HOW TO WRITE POSTS THAT GO VIRAL WITHOUT SELLING OUT

Attract A Raving Fan Base, Understand Your First Viral Hit, And Discover Your Unique Blogging Voice

Contents

CHAPTER ONE: DISCOVERING YOUR UNIQUE BLOGGING VOICE 2

CHAPTER TWO: DISCOVERING AND ATTRACTING YOUR IDEAL FAN BASE 6

CHAPTER THREE: IDEAS TO GET YOU STARTED 14

CHAPTER FOUR: THE SECRET KEYS TO ENGAGING BLOG POSTS THAT GO VIRAL 21

CHAPTER FIVE: PROFITABILITY MATTERS TOO 25

CHAPTER SIX: VIRAL GROWTH 29

CHAPTER SEVEN: CONCLUSION 33

CHAPTER ONE: DISCOVERING YOUR UNIQUE BLOGGING VOICE

Before we get into the specifics of how you can write blog posts that get your readers hooked to your blog and always come back wanting for more, let me ask you one simple question – **What attracts you to a particular blog?**

Think for a few seconds and answer the following questions:

- Was it the content? Was the content REALLY amazing and unique?
- Was it the unique talent to captivate readers that the blog owner possesses?
- Or, was it the manner in which the blog post was written?

In a majority of cases the third question would have an affirmative answer. You read a particular person's blog post because you want to read their opinion, understand their perspective <u>and are in love with the manner in which they write</u>.

How does this happen?

How can this person know what readers want?

And more important, how can they write exactly what the readers want?

You sometimes refer to these people as '<u>gifted writers</u>' or '<u>born writers</u>.'

The fact however is that these people are completely natural – they have learnt the art of embracing who they really are and are now sharing their ideas with the whole world!

Is it that simple?

Yes, it is! <u>These 'natural, gifted writers' have discovered their unique blogging voice and this is what draws you towards them</u>.

So, **what is a unique blogging voice?**

Well, a unique blogging voice is the voice that you use to share your opinion with others. It is the courage that you demonstrate to share stuff that you are afraid to share. It is the boldness to share your secrets and stories.

It is unique to you and resonates with your readers. Remember, it does not have to resonate with everybody around there – it is okay if it only resonates with a select group of people. However, it is important that this voice resonates DEEPLY with this particular group of people.

And the most important part – you do not have to find your unique blogging voice. <u>It finds you! It is already there – within you!</u>

All you need is the courage to start. You should not let your insecurities, doubts and fears stop you.

But I am not a great writer?

So what? No one is – initially.

If I talk about myself, my writing style has evolved over the years – I do not write the way I would write three years back and in the next five years, I am sure that my writing style may be different to what it is today.

The point here is that in order to discover your amazing blogging voice, you need to take action – every single day. This means that you will need to write without any fear or doubt every single day. Just let go of your fears that limit your expressions and be amazed at the writer in you making a difference in people's lives.

You must remember that your readers want to hear your opinion, they are reading your blog because they believe in you. They believe that you are authentic and want to gain from your perspective.

But other bloggers write much better than me?

Must be – but then they have been blogging for years, haven't they? Do not let your inner critic undermine you. Let this critic be the fuel that you need for your writing.

And – do not compare yourself. NEVER.

The only thing that should matter for you is that you are moving ahead, learning something new every day, improving every day and having fun during the process.

Even if your writing sucks today, focus on improving it – the only way to do this is by writing every day. Do let your self-limiting doubts hamper your confidence.

And do not feel obligated to agree to other people's opinion.

Your readers are reading your blog because they like your unique blogging voice – which is a voice full of strength, authenticity and truthfulness.

<u>Actions steps:</u>

The main actionable from this chapter is to begin writing every single day. Ideally, you should be writing a short blog post every day (around 500 words). It's not important to publish it yet – in fact, do not publish it till the time you are not 100% convinced that you want to. And the voice in your head will tell you when you are ready to publish.

Remember, there are no rules – in order to discover your writing voice, you can write about anything – ranging from fashion to medicine to crocheting to parenting to…the list is endless. Pick up what inspires you most and just get started.

CHAPTER TWO: DISCOVERING AND ATTRACTING YOUR IDEAL FAN BASE

How do you normally write?

You think about a topic and get started, correct?

Most of us write like that.

Isn't that how it should be?

No, because people who deploy a different strategy than this one always tend to achieve better success.

This is because these people or 'the natural, gifted writers' write for a special someone. They write for their ideal reader or fan base.

Their fan base strengthens their writing power.

The idea here is to focus on your ideal readers and write for them – that way you are writing for a special someone and not risking generating boring blog posts.

So, where are these ideal readers found?

They are found everywhere – they are the people who read your blog. They are the ones who will come back to your blog and they are the ones who will get more traffic on your blog by liking and commenting on your post.

But I am just starting out? I do not have a fan base of readers? Who do I write for?

Well, you do have a fan base of hungry readers who are waiting to read your next blog post. And that is why we call this chapter as 'discovering' your ideal fan base and not 'creating' you fan base. <u>They are already there</u>! You just have to attract them!

How can I discover them?

Think about who you are writing for. Some important factors to be considered are their gender, age, marital status, likes and dislikes, view point, income, etc.

You just need to keep these people in mind as you write your blog posts. It is always a great idea to imagine them sitting next to you and asking as many questions as they can. Ideally, your blog post should be able to provide all the answers.

If you are still unsure, think about a past version of yourself as your ideal reader. Nobody understands your struggles better than you. All you need to do is go back in time and think about the difficulties that you faced. Could you create a blog post talking about all those difficulties?

You want to make sure that other people (your potential readers) learn from your mistakes.

Try and understand what your ideal reader wants. If your ideal fan base is a past version of your own self, think about what kind of knowledge or insight you would have appreciated when you started out.

If the subject of your blog is travel, think about the things that you would have liked when you began your journey as an avid traveler. Would you have loved some travel tips? May be some tips to save money as you travel? Would you have appreciated mini travel guides that you could print and take along to your place of travel? May be a travel guide with prices of hotels and eating outlets?

Think about the kind of information that would have eased your life.

That is the kind of information that your ideal reader wants! **And by providing this information, you convert your readers into your fans.**

Just remember to keep things simple and not overwhelm your fan base.

But where do I start?

Well, stat by thinking about the challenges your potential fan base is facing. Taking the above example of a travel related blog: Do your readers know from where they can procure discounted tickets for museums and art galleries? Do they know the various options that they have in case they are looking at long term travel- in fact, they could travel for free? Would they like to know if they need to carry eatables (depending on the place where they are going to be travelling)? Would they need a list of some government run hospitals and pharmacies where they could visit in case of an emergency? Do they understand the concept of travel insurance? Do they need to buy special things to travel with children?

As you begin jotting down the challenges, you realize that you have more than enough content. Right?

But if I write only about travel, won't I be restricting my fan base?

Yes, but that is the idea – you are in the process of discovering your fan base, and **once you have discovered them, they will stick to you**. So if you are writing for a special someone, let's name this person as Robin – then Robin and everybody like Robin will read your blog – eventually, you will dominate the market. And that's the real idea – you are writing for your fan base – only the people who want to read what you write.

INSPIRE YOUR FAN BASE

Imagine your ideal reader, Robin arriving on your website and seeing the following blog posts:

- Travel guide to Spain
- Luxury travel experience to Switzerland
- Places to visit in Florida
- Great food joint in Gold Coast
- Australia – the food, the education and the culture
- A trip to the Taj Mahal, India
- A summer trip to Valencia, Spain

How would Robin feel? Would she want to visit your website again?

I bet not – and the reason is simple: **Your travel blog is not addressing any of Robin's needs!**

But I don't know what her needs are!

I get that – and that is why it is important to think about the information that YOU needed when you started to travel.

Think of your past experiences and create posts that readers can relate to. They want their problems solved, they don't want a bunch of posts that you like.

How about dividing your blog into different sections?

Now, imagine Robin visits your site and notices the following sections:

- Travel tips for beginners
- Budget family vacations
- Honeymoon travel destinations
- Adventure travel destinations
- Summer holiday trips
- Beautiful beaches
- Rocky mountains
- Earn as you travel

As she clicks on a section, she gets a list of topics under each section. This could be something like

Travel tips for beginners

- Twelve things you cannot ignore as you plan your next travel
- Five important tips for first time travelers
- Things to carry along during your travel
- Child friendly travel destinations and hotels
- Five Budget hotel options in each country
- The dilemma of public vs private conveyance – which one, where and why?
- Fifteen tips that ensure that your cash is safe as you travel
- Twenty seven ways to save money as you travel
- Ten proven ways to earn money as you travel
- How to achieve maximum fun with family?

- How to travel alone and yet have fun?
- Hotel or homestay – deciding on the best option and exercising caution?

Wouldn't this want her to come back to your website?

The key to inspire your readers is to tell inspiring stories. Most blogs provide dozens of tips but do not provide information on where to start from and what to do with those tips. You have an advantage here – you have applied all these tips when you started out!

Use your experience to your advantage, share your flaws, talk about things that you did right – inspire your readers!

Inspiring people is not about making them feel good. You must understand that as you inspire your readers and help them reach their goals, you help yourself too!

You need to show them that you have been there, done that and that if you could do it, they can too.

Here is my proven process to inspire your fan base:

UNDERSTAND THEIR PROBLEM: Begin the process by identifying what your readers are struggling with and what information would they wish to have. As an example, somebody who plans to travel the world, would need information on planning their travel itinerary, procuring travel tickets, exploring various boarding and lodging options, understanding the culture of places they would visit, using the best resources to save money while travelling, etc.

Remember how confused you were when you got started and begin by helping the past version of your own self.

NARRATE YOUR HONEST STORY: Talk about your frustrations, things that you wanted to do and were not able to, things that you wish you knew back then.

And then...*share how you overcome all hurdles, how you persevered to reach your goals and how your readers can also achieve their goals by following a few simple tips.*

SHARE USEFUL AND PRACTICAL TIPS: In this section, get into the details of your story, talk about your problems and mention specific tips on how you overcame all hurdles. Share your mistakes and talk about lessons you learnt from them. This will help your fan base in relating to your post.

ALWAYS END ON A HIGH: This is very important. While you tell Robin how she will make mistakes and learn from them, it is also important to provide her the comfort that things will be fine and that she will enjoy the process. She must be able to visualize the fun that she is going to have after all the struggle and hard work.

This is what will inspire her to take action and come back to your website – to read the same post again or to look for new ones.

ACTION ITEMS:

So, the action items from this chapter are:

- Think about your ideal reader or fan base. You could even give them a name or visualize a past version of your own self as your ideal reader.
- Write down the problems that your potential fan base encounters.
- Identify these with your own personal story.
- Tell your story and inspire your readers in the post.
- Always end on a high note, inspiring them to take action.

CHAPTER THREE: IDEAS TO GET YOU STARTED

Do you ever fear that you may run out of ideas?

Well, it is actually impossible to come up with original ideas every week without getting any help. But here is my strategy for you – you must follow specific formulas that are deployed by other successful bloggers. That way, the content that you publish is proven to work.

The internet is flooded with information promising blog post ideas. In reality, you just need to publish the kind of posts your ideal reader wants to read. This way you are sure to get an engaged fan base.

According to me, all blog posts fall in either one of the below mentioned categories:

THE MASSIVE VALUE BLOG POSTS: As the name suggests, these posts add massive value to the readers – these are the posts that your readers crave to read. They simply love these ones and can't wait for more such content. It takes time to create these posts but always keep in mind that these posts can do amazing things to build your readership.

THE FILLER POSTS: These are the shorter articles that you see on most blogs. It is important to understand that your filler posts should provide as much value as your massive value blog posts. It is best to talk about at least one action item that readers can immediately apply after reading a filler post.

Let us now look at a few ideas that can get you started:

Before going to the ideas section, I want you to reexamine your ultimate goal – *you want a thoroughly engaged fan base and therefore want to write content that other marketers would sell.* The secret key to doing this is to create insane value through your post.

Here are some ideas to help you write your massive value blog posts:

Idea 1: Publish content that provides tons of value and become your ideal reader's one stop solution provider: You want to publish content that other marketers would sell. This also implies that you become the problem solver. The best thing is to provide a detailed solution to any major problem your ideal fan base would be facing and then make it available for free. So, here are the things that must be considered as you create content for this kind of a post:

- Your post must provide step by step solutions
- Adding videos, screenshots and images can add more value to the post
- Talking about obstacles that you have encountered can inspire your readers
- Links to related resources from experts on the field are a bonus

A blog post that addresses all the above mentioned points ensures that it provides utility. Your post must provide an immediately implementable blueprint.

Here are some examples of titles that you could use:

- Your fifteen minute guide to making real money online
- How to use Amazon to your advantage
- The guide to purchasing your first DSLR camera
- The five minute guide to achieve mutual satisfaction in bed

Idea two: Use a numbered list to provide information: A number of people find the idea of numbered lists as cliché. However, if you do it correctly, you are sure to grab instant attention in any niche. Numbered lists could simply be a collection of some useful resources. They could even be a compilation of tips or an assortment of bite sized chunks of information. All you need to do is to create a list of what your potential fan base wants. Here are some examples of titles for these kinds of posts:

- 51 great tips to beat the procrastination habit
- 101 ways to win the woman of your dreams
- 40 websites to help you save money while travelling
- 25 best courses to choose from at Harvard
- Top 30 universities in the world

Idea three: Use case studies to win credibility: A case study is a detailed breakdown of how you have overcome a particular situation, using a specialized technique. This is a post that demonstrates proof of something working or not working.

Readers love these posts because it provides them a step by step plan of something that works. All they have to do is follow the blueprint that is mentioned in the post.

Some examples of titles for these posts are:

- How I used the power of my mind to overcome Fibromyalgia
- How I wrote a non-fiction e-book in 20 days
- My 30 day weight loss challenge
- How to use social media to generate $100 dollars extra income every single day

Idea four: Write a series: A series of blog posts can combine the best of both worlds – it provides real life examples of case studies along with some great solutions to problems that readers face.

You could provide regular updates to track the progress of a niche specific topic.

You could publish chapter wise posts where you pick up a massive topic and provide bite sized updates.

You could even provide updates about a topic as and when you learn something new.

Some examples of titles for such kind of posts are:

- The perfect guide to self-branding (Chapter based)
- Mastering Microsoft excel in 11 days
- 30 day decluttering challenge

And now let us look at ideas that can help you write filler posts that engage readers:

Idea five: Posts explaining your mindset: Let us understand this – people visit your blog because they like to read what you write – which implies that they like your perspective. An excellent way to increase reader engagement is to create a set of beliefs via your posts. It is not important for your readers to agree on everything that you write. The important thing is that they understand what you stand for. Mindset posts are the easiest to write. All you need to do is think about a particular topic and provide your opinion on that.

Title examples include:

- Why leaning in is important?
- Godfather in career – today's corporate reality!
- The truth about intermittent fasting

Idea six: Definition posts: These ones are pretty simple to create too. Most bloggers make the mistake of thinking that their readers understand all the terms that they use in their massive value blog posts. They could pick up certain terms from these blog posts and create fresh filler posts, defining the terms used.

Examples include:

- What is the urgent important matrix after all?
- What do you mean by passive income?
- The importance of 'location independence.'

Idea seven: Product reviews: People are on your site because they value your opinion. Use this to your advantage by providing reviews about specific products that you feel strongly about. Write about what products can work and what would not work according to you. Provide affiliate links to the product and earn easy money.

Examples of such posts include:

- The best anti-wrinkle cream that I found at a local drugstore

- My review of the new Murphy Richards OTG
- Do nootropics actually work?

Idea eight: Narrate inspiring stories: Stories have been around since ages. Talk about a valuable lesson that you learnt via short stories and inspire your fan base. All you need to remember is to create passion in your writing. Stories possess a unique ability to evoke emotions and capture the attention of the audience. The stories that you narrate can go a long way in strengthening your relationship with your readers. Some examples of titles for these posts are:

- My cancer story – How I beat lung cancer naturally
- Things that I did wrong with my Mr. Right
- Lessons that I learnt about work life balance – the hard way

Idea nine: Interview an expert: Readers love to read about influential people. Think about the leaders in your particular niche and send a set of questions for them to answer. Make sure you ask questions that they do not get asked otherwise.

Examples of such blog posts include:

- Tim Morrison's perspective on the magic of thinking big
- Amanda Simmons – why she loves clutter, clutter and more clutter
- Sudha Kochhar – the reasons she hates her profession

Idea ten: Lessons from celebrities: Let's face this – we live in a celebrity obsessed culture. You can use this fact to your advantage. Take some time to research about some key learnings or interesting facts about the celebrities in your niche and craft a compelling post that entices readers. Some title examples are:

- How Sheryl Sandberg learnt to Lean in – the true story of a woman leader in a male dominated world
- Roger Federer talks about things not to do before a match – Lessons from the God of Tennis
- Ten easy ways to destroy your personal brand – Lance Armstrong!

Action steps:

And now let us look at the action steps from this chapter:

The most important action step here is to create three blog post – one massive value blog post and two filler posts. It is alright if you do not do well – do not publish your post till the time you are one hundred percent satisfied with what you have written. Write, rewrite and rewrite – just make sure that you are writing every single day – so that you are able to discover your unique blogging voice and engage a fan base of lovely readers.

CHAPTER FOUR: THE SECRET KEYS TO ENGAGING BLOG POSTS THAT GO VIRAL

I am sure that you have your unique blogging style. A number of individuals prefer to flavor the article with their distinct personality whereas some choose to write simple 'how-to' articles without caring about the likeability factor.

No matter how you write, it is important to include some key factors in your post. These secret keys possess the capability to entice readers:

Secret key one: Each blog post should have a compelling headline: You must ensure that the headline that you use for your blog post grabs loads of attention. Think about headlines that your readers care about – what keeps them up at night, what are their greatest fears, what are some of the immediate takeaways for them from this post, what are they most inquisitive about, etc. Some title examples are:

- How safe is your dedicated husband from the secretary who is known to be a flirt?
- 5 Warning signs that you are about to get fired
- Can you trust PayPal?
- How your orthopedist is putting you at a risk of bone cancer: 5 ways to protect yourself NOW!
- Parenting alert: seven steps to hire the next babysitter
- 10 things no one will tell you about investment banking

- Warning – the truth about over the counter analgesics!

Secret key two: Each blog post should begin with a hook statement: Yes, I am saying that the beginning of your blog post MUST be impressive. Use the first paragraph to grab attention. Your goal is to sell value to your readers and provide them with a reason to continue reading your post.

Think about lines that can get them hooked to the post and include these lines in the very first paragraph.

Secret key three: Use short paragraphs: Research proves that people like to read content that is available in bite sized chunks. Whenever possible, limit the number of lines in a paragraph to four or five. This may break certain grammar rules but is sure to grab attention.

Secret key four: Use images wisely: It is always good to use an image in your post. The best way to do this is by right aligning the image.

This forces your readers to move down and look at the content below, which in turn increases the time that they spend on your website. (sometimes, minor things count too!)

Secret key five: Make your blog post solution focused: And promise this in the beginning of your post. Well, once your readers are hooked, they will continue to read further. Therefore, it is important to offer the promise of a solution right in the beginning. Discuss the problem statement, talk about how and why you understand their problem and offer a solution which will be presented in the bulk of the article.

Secret key six: Optimize your post for keywords: You must ensure that any blog post that you write contains a primary keyword that you are targeting. This will ensure that you get enough traffic from people who are searching the net for these keywords. Include keywords in places such as title, URL, subtitle and the first paragraph.

Secret key seven: Interlink your posts: Once you have a reader on your blog, you want them to stick around for some time. The best way to do this is by interlinking related content on your site. You can choose the number of links that you want to use. I prefer up to five links but never go beyond that. The reason is that I do not want my blog post to simply look like a bunch of links.

Secret key eight: Ensure that your blog post is easy to scan:This is extremely important. You must ensure that the complete blogpost grabs instant attention. In order to do this, ensure that your post:

- Has a compelling headline
- Is broken down into small paragraphs
- Contains a catch phrase that grabs instant attention
- Include bolded statements that readers look at immediately
- Includes a catchy image

Just use all these points and you will be able to create a magical blogpost in no time.

Secret key nine: Provide an action plan: Towards the end of the post, especially the posts where you want your readers to learn something new, provide clear steps that they can implement. Tell your readers what to do next and how you will be able to help. This will increase engagement and ensure that they check future articles on your website.

Secret key ten: Conclude your post with an engagement building question: It is important to seek reader feedback and let your readers know that you value what they are saying and want to make every effort to ensure that their needs are met. The best way to do this is by soliciting feedback at the end of the post. Ask your readers to comment or voice their opinion on the subject. This is an excellent way to build a personal connection with your readers.

ACTION STEPS:

And now, here are the action items from this chapter:

I would like you to go back and look at the posts that you have written previously. Analyze each post to see if it contains the ten secret ingredients of a great blog post. If it does not, rewrite the post once again.

Now, writing a great blog post that your readers enjoy is a skill that you have learnt. All that is required is mastering this skill by consistent practice.

CHAPTER FIVE: PROFITABILITY MATTERS TOO

By now, you have a list of ideas that can help you build reader engagement. You have also unlocked the secret keys to writing great blog posts.

The next thing that needs to be done is to understand blogging as a business and pick up niche that is profitable. Here are some simple steps to accomplish that:

Keyword research matters: Keyword research enables people to discover the basic demand for a particular blog idea. Google's Keyword Planner tool is an excellent resource here. You could also use the Google's suggestion tool.

You aim is to eliminate any idea that does not get at least a few thousand exact searches every month.

Competition matters: The thing about competition is that there are multiple people using the same blog idea and yet making money. You, too can be one of them. Remember, there are thousand ways to stand out in a competitive environment.

How can you determine if your blog topic has competition?

Well simply answer the following questions:

- Are there other blogs available on this topic?
- Is this topic covered in some YouTube videos or iTunes podcasts?

- Is there a Facebook page related to this topic?
- Do any advertisements pop up when you research this topic on Google?

All these factors demonstrate a significant amount of competition. Absence of these factors indicates a weak market with no competition.

Affiliate products matter too: Affiliate marketing is one of the best ways to monetize a blog. An important strategy that can get you immediate profits is to find an existing affiliate product that you can recommend to your audience. However, you must take time to research the affiliate products. Remember, there are hundreds of them there. Therefore, you might need to do a little digging to research a quality offer.

Information sells: Yes, specific 'how-to' blogs do very well sometimes. Once again, the key is to take time with your research and identify a specific information focused niche. In order to draw immediate profitability, I suggest using the Amazon.com top keywords section. Check out the top books that come up in your research and use these as affiliate links. Make sure that you recommend books that have a rank under 20,000.

Solving multiple problems also helps: If you are able to solve multiple problems within one niche, and you also notice a demand for that niche through the Google search tools – well, you have hit the jackpot!

An example could be a travel related blog offering multiple solutions such as:

- How to save on eating out during your travel to Australia?
- How to discover the best last minute discounts for your travel?
- How to decide on sight-seeing options during your travel?

Another example could be a career women centric niche. A women career oriented blog could look at addressing multiple issues such as:

- Why are mentors so important in career progression?
- Mentors or sponsors – the truth about career progression
- Eyeing the corner office? Ten easy ways to make it happen!

Passionate audience is important too: The niche that you venture into MUST have an already engaged and passionate audience. The key to find passionate people is to look for people who talk about this topic on Facebook or Twitter, join some network groups related to the topic, read and comment on the existing blogs in this market and buy magazines related to the niche.

Now, all the above steps can enable you to determine the profitability of your blog. However, you do not need all seven to succeed. Sometimes, the idea that you are passionate about may not have tons of affiliate offers. This does not mean that the idea should be shelved. The most important thing is discovering a market that is full of passionate ideas.

ACTION STEPS:

The main action step from this chapter is to look for a niche that you are passionate about and that helps you accomplish at least some of your profitability goals.

You now understand the niche where you want to stay and you are also equipped to write blog posts that can keep your audience hooked.

Let's get started!

CHAPTER SIX: VIRAL GROWTH

By now, you have mastered the art of writing blog posts for an engaged audience as well as finding profitable niches.

But I want to take my blog to the next level?

Sure, and for that – you need viral traffic, correct?

Let us first try and understand the definition of going viral. For some people, a blog post may be considered as viral if it has at least a million views. Others may not be so rigid about numbers. Personally, I am not rigid about numbers – for me viral growth is something that implies a large number of people sharing my content through social media. You could say that it is '*word of mouth marketing using social media as one of the catalysts.*'

YOUR UNIQUE BLOGGING VOICE MATTERS!

Yes, for a blog post to go viral, you must write great content in your unique blogging voice. You must understand that viral blog traffic is amazing and if you are able to capture it through the use of the right kind of blogging voice, your blog can grow exponentially. If people love your voice, they will share your content – this also implies that your content can only go viral only if it is awesome. Yes, *you must write great content in your authentic blogging voice.*

TARGETING THE RIGHT SOCIAL MEDIA SITES MATTERS TOO!

Today, the social media is flooded with various options – Facebook, Twitter, Google+, Pinterest, LinkedIn, Instagram, Reddit, etc.

Personally, since we are looking at your blog as a business and are concerned about profitability too, we will evaluate your time on social media in terms of Return on Investment.

Imagine you have a million followers on Twitter!

Now, **what is the point if they don't read your blog regularly?**

My suggestion to you here is to figure out where your audience is and build your presence there. If you are targeting a niche that involves young, dynamic job seekers, then LinkedIn is the place to develop your presence in.

If your blog targets housewives or stay at home moms, Pinterest is the ideal option.

Spend some time in completing your research on which social media platform is most used by the people you are targeting and build your presence there.

STRATEGY MATTERS!

Yes, and you must take time to build your social media strategy. You cannot simply post one post today and another after two weeks and then the next one after a day followed by no post for a month!

A smarter approach here is to take time to develop your long term strategy and create a plan that includes regular updates and posts. So, instead of randomly posting three updates on three consecutive days and then getting frustrated by not posting anything for three consecutive weeks, it is best to have a plan that allows you to post regular updates every single day. Some sites have specific tools that allow you to post updates. Facebook's scheduling tool is one such option.

VISUAL APPEAL MATTERS!

It is important that the content that is posted on social media sites is of the highest quality. Remember to use great quality photos for all your posts. Visual appeal matters a lot.

Smart use of Pinterest can help you convert users into readers. The main goal of Pinterest is to share great content. Some things to remember as you use Pinterest and Facebook are:

Improve your homepage – It is great if your home page mentions the name of your blog. That's the way readers will recognize you. Take some time to craft out a personal description – make sure it is likeable and awesome. And that it captures your unique blogging voice – because that will help you discover your ideal fan base.

Work on your boards – Your Pinterest boards must demonstrate what you and your blog are all about. You can divide your boards into niche specific categories – the more, the merrier! Ensure that you have a 'Best of my blog' kind of a board out there to captivate your readers.

Establish a personal connection – Your readers or the ideal fan base from social media sites must acknowledge that there is a REAL person behind each post. Include your headshot at some prominent place on your home page and include a link to the blog somewhere close. Create links to your most awesome content and highlight popular posts.

Offer an incentive – Offer an incentive for email subscribers. A short e-book is generally the best incentive that can be offered. Try and connect with your e mail subscribers regularly to create a connection.

And now, here is your action plan from this chapter:

- Stop trying to create an active presence on all the social media sites available.
- Create a definite marketing strategy for the sites that you are targeting.
- Improve your homepage and make sure that your blog name matches your user name.
- Ensure that your best posts have some great images that engage readers almost instantly.
- Work on converting new visitors into regular blog readers.

CHAPTER SEVEN: CONCLUSION

If you are not determined to blog, you will probably give up much before your blog gains traction. And there is absolutely nothing wrong with that. You were trying to something that you did not want to!

However, if you are aiming at building a successful blog, you must realize that it takes time. Writing blog posts that can generate some profit and engage audience simultaneously is a skill that can be mastered with time. Ultimately, these are the blog posts that generate viral traffic and empower exponential blog growth.

It is a continuous process of discovering what works and then channelizing your energies and efforts to ensure that it does work.

Remember, there may be initial challenges and you may want to quit. However, only the determined few will be able to move forward even when the going gets tough. These challenges will only shape you as a blogger and contribute to your success.

So, embrace them as a gift and continue to enjoy the process of blogging. Use these as opportunities to create your next blog post and gather more engagement. That is the only way to get viral traffic!

Listen to your motivation and enjoy the ride.

All the best!

Before You Go…

Thank you again for downloading this book!

I hope this book was able to help give you an understanding of how to write great blog posts that go viral and create a raving fan base.

Finally, if you enjoyed this book, then I'd like to ask you for a favor, would you be kind enough to leave a review for this book on Amazon? It'd be greatly appreciated!

Check Out My Other Books

Below you'll find one of my other #1 Amazon bestseller books that is popular on Amazon and Kindle as well.

How To Start A Profitable Blog: A Guide To Create Content That Rocks, Build Traffic, And Turn Your Blogging Passion Into Profit.

http://www.amazon.com/How-Blog-Profit-Step---Step-ebook/dp/B00ZVE2G8E

When you Download *How To Start A Profitable Blog: A Guide To Create Content That Rocks, Build Traffic, And Turn Your Blogging Passion Into Profit*, you'll learn everything you need to know about how to blog:

- What Blogging is All About

- How to Get Started

- The Costs Involved

- Blogging Platforms

- What You Should Write About

And Much More! Grab Your Copy Today, **for FREE. Read on your PC, Mac, Smartphone, Tablet, or Kindle Device- Download Your Copy Today!**

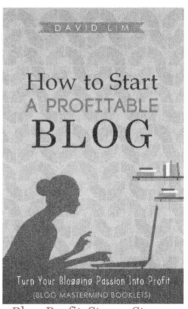

http://www.amazon.com/How-Blog-Profit-Step---Step-ebook/dp/B00ZVE2G8E

Printed in Great Britain
by Amazon